"Quique dati leto quaeque dedere fleo."

College of S. Columba

ET SIMPLICES SICVT COLVMBÆ PRVDENTES SICVT SERPENTES

ROLL OF HONOUR

1914-1918.

Published by

The Old Columban Society.

Foreword.

TO every one of our readers the War Roll, which the Old Columban Society presents, must bring sadness. The price is heavy, even for the undying glory in which, as these pages prove, the College of St. Columba has claimed her share. The sympathy of all Columbans will go out to the parents, family, and friends of those whose names are here enshrined among the fallen. But for them, as for us all, the first and final thought will be pride—pride for the School which has taught her sons so well, and pride for the sons who have been so nobly true to her teaching.

The College of St. Columba has sent throughout her history a large proportion of her best to the Army and Navy; but it was something more than a military tradition which impelled many whose names stand on our list. They had caught the spirit of their School, and, therefore, they knew where duty lay.

Out of 880 Old Columbans living who entered S. C. C. since 1870 no less than 385 have found a way to serve. They came from the homeland, they came from the far ends of the earth, because their ears were open to the voice of honour. 65 Old Columbans and 5 ex-Masters have made the great sacrifice, and 2 have been reported as "missing"; 71 have been wounded, many of them more than once.

Among the distinctions and decorations which have been won are the following:—C.B. (6), C.I.E. (1), C.M.G. (7), D.S.O. (24), Bar to D.S.O. (1), Legion of Honour (5), Croix de Guerre (5), Military Cross (30), Bar to Military Cross (1), Mentioned in Despatches (66). Truly a noble record, and while no pains have been spared to make the Roll complete, we ask pardon for any inadvertent omissions which may have occurred.

We are deeply grateful to Mrs. Blackburn for her untiring efforts in obtaining photographs of Old Columbans on active service, and it is from this collection we have been enabled to procure the photographs which appear in this volume of those O.C.'s on active service who have fallen.

The task of raising a permanent Memorial at the College now remains, and a sub-Committee has been appointed to collect funds. It is a debt of honour to Old Columbans, and particularly to those of us who at home have been spared all the horrors and dangers of war, to ensure by their ungrudging support that the Memorial in its character, scope and design is truly worthy of the men and ideals which it is desired to perpetuate.

E. A. RICE, O. C. *Editor,*
Landore, Dodder Road, Rathgar.

CECIL L. SMITH, *Hon. Treasurer,*
25 Merrion Square, Dublin.

May, 1919.

1. GEORGE CASTRIOT DE RINZY (1878). 2. EDWARD LEIGH (1879).
3. RICHARD E. PHILLIPS GABBETT (1880). 4. CHARLES RODNEY WOLFE SPEDDING (1885).

Roll of Honour.

FELLOWS.

Brigadier-General Lord Ardee, D.S.O., Irish Guards. *Companion of the Order of the Bath. Mentioned in Despatches. Twice Wounded.*

Major the Earl of Pembroke, Royal Horse Guards (General Headquarters' Staff). *Mentioned in Despatches.*

Captain Sir Stanley Cochrane, Bart. (1893), 7th Battalion Royal Dublin Fusiliers.

Captain E. H. Alton, F.T.C.D., Dublin University Officers' Training Corps. *Military Cross.*

Sergeant G. Fitzgibbon, Dublin University Officers' Training Corps.

Major A. C. O'Sullivan, F.T.C.D., Royal Army Medical Corps.

MASTERS.

Captain J. N. Treble, 5th Battalion Oxford and Bucks Light Infantry. *Killed in action.*

Lieutenant P. F. Cross, 4th Battalion Royal Irish Regiment (attached 6th Battalion). *Killed in action November, 1916.*

Second Lieutenant J. A. H. Taylor, 1st Battalion Royal Dublin Fusiliers. *Killed in action 24th September, 1915.*

Second Lieutenant J. S. West, Royal Garrison Artillery. *Killed in action July, 1916.*

Lieutenant T. E. Sanderson, 4th Battalion York and Lancaster Regiment. *Killed in action 13th April, 1918.*

Rev. P. S. Whelan (Warden, 1891-1904), Chaplain to the Forces.

Captain R. Magill, 3rd Battalion Royal Irish Fusiliers (attached 2nd Battalion). *Wounded.*

Captain B. W. Burton, 7th Officers' Cadet Battalion.

Lieutenant-Colonel H. Aplin, 7th Battalion Royal Munster Fusiliers. *Distinguished Service Order. Croix de Chevalier du Légion d'Honneur. Mentioned in Despatches. Wounded.*

Lieutenant W. A. Ellis, 15th Battalion Royal Irish Rifles.

Lieutenant J. G. Fitzmaurice, 7th Battalion Royal Munster Fusiliers. *Mentioned in Despatches. Wounded.*

Captain A. A. Luce, 12th Battalion Royal Irish Rifles. *Military Cross.*

Second Lieutenant H. W. Wilmot, Royal Engineers.

Lieutenant W. H. Murphy, 2nd King's African Rifles. *Twice wounded.*

Captain R. St. G. Johnston, 3rd Battalion Royal Irish Regiment. *Wounded.*

Lieutenant W. A. Bell, Officers' Training Corps.

Lieutenant C. F. H. Tacchella, Indian Army.

Lance-Corporal W. E. Bishop, 2/7th Battalion The Black Watch.

Rev. W. H. Skene, Chaplain, Remount Depôt, Army Service Corps.

Major R. W. Tate, Commanding Dublin University Officers' Training Corps.

Private F. C. Butcher, University of Toronto Officers' Training Corps, Overseas Company, C.E.F.

Second-Lieutenant W. G. Pontet, Officers' Training Corps, S.C.C.

1. ARTHURE BENEDICT EDWARD HILLAS (1887). 2. CHARLES OWEN SLACKE (1888).
3. JAMES ROWAN SHAW (1892). 4. WILLIAM MAXWELL SHAW (1892)

OLD COLUMBANS.

1855.

Colonel Charles F. C. Beresford, 7th Battalion Surrey Volunteer Regiment, 1915-18.

1862.

Lieutenant-Colonel J. E. Jameson, Commanding 24th Battalion City of London Regiment (The Queen's).

Commander the Hon. F. Spring-Rice, Royal Navy, Coast Defence.

1865.

Colonel H. F. Lyons-Montgomery, C.B., Military Member of Travelling Medical Board, Southern Command.

1867.

Major E. Lindsay, Recruiting Officer, Bolton, Lancashire.

1869.

Colonel Sir William A. Johns. *Companion of the Order of the Bath. Commander of the Order of the Empire of India. Mentioned in Despatches. Died of illness contracted while on active service.*

1870.

Colonel W. R. H. Beresford-Ash, 10th Battalion Royal Welsh Fusiliers. *Wounded.*

1871.

Colonel D. St. J. Grant, Indian Medical Service.

Brigadier-General V. T. Bunbury, C.B., D.S.O., General Headquarters' Staff. Provost Marshal. *Companion of the Order of SS. Michael and George. Commandeur de l'Ordre de la Couronne. Mentioned in Despatches.*

Brigadier-General W. E. Bunbury, C.B., Quartermaster-General, Indian Army.

Major H. H. M. O'Grady, 8th Battalion Royal Sussex Regiment.

Lieutenant-Colonel L. T. Bowles, Commanding 1st Battalion Royal Militia of the Island of Jersey.

Major-General W. Fry, C.B., C.V.O., in Charge of Administration in Ireland. *Mentioned in Despatches.*

Colonel J. S. Brown, Commanding 8th Battalion Royal Irish Fusiliers. *Mentioned in Despatches.*

Colonel C. Garner, Royal Army Medical Corps, Visiting and Inspecting Medical Officer of Prisoners of War Camps and Hospitals in Egypt and Cyprus. *Mentioned in Despatches. Commander of the Order of the British Empire (Mil. Div.). Knight of Grace, Order of the Hospital of St. John of Jerusalem.*

1872.

Captain H. A. Richey, 12th Battalion Royal Inniskilling Fusiliers.

1873.

Captain J. V. Manning, South African Medical Corps.

Colonel W. M. Ellis, Royal Engineers.

Rev. G. H. Andrews, Chaplain, 88th Victoria Fusiliers, British Columbia.

1. AUBREY ULICK O'BRIEN (1893). 2. VIVIAN ALFRED BARTON (1894).
3. CHARLES ERSKINE BARTON (1894). 4. THOMAS VILLIERS THACKER NEVILLE (1895).

1875.

Lieutenant-Commander H. B. Boothby, Royal Naval Reserve. *Distinguished Service Order.*

Major E. W. Guinness, Royal Engineers.

1876.

Captain S. L. Gwynn, 6th Battalion Connaught Rangers. *Croix de Chevalier du Légion d'Honneur.*

Captain S. C. G. F. Astell, D.S.O., General Staff Officer, 2nd Grade.

1877.

Rev. R. S. Deane Oliver, Deputy Assistant Chaplain-General to the Forces. *Mentioned in Despatches.*

Captain Sir A. H. Armstrong, Bart., The Connaught Rangers.

District Superintendent J. P. Algie, Imperial Police Service, Burmah.

Lieutenant-Colonel J. R. Wolfe, late 3rd Battalion Royal Irish Regiment. Staff Lieutenant, Headquarters' Staff.

1878.

Colonel G. C. de Rinzy, Commanding Local Forces British Guiana. *Died of illness contracted while on active service.*

Lieutenant-Colonel J. D. Alexander, Royal Army Medical Corps, Assistant Director of Medical Services. *Distinguished Service Order. Officier de l'Ordre de Léopold.*

Colonel E. P. J. F. Macartney-Filgate, 12th Battalion Lancashire Fusiliers.

1879.

Major E. Leigh, 2nd Battalion Hampshire Regiment. *Killed in action 2nd May, 1915.*

Brigadier-General R. O. Kellett, Commanding 99th Infantry Brigade. *Companion of the Order of the Bath. Companion of the Order of SS. Michael and George. Three times mentioned in Despatches.*

Major J. E. Carter, Royal Army Medical Corps.

Major J. H. Davidson-Houston, Special Reserve.

Lieutenant-Colonel P. Peacock, Royal Marine Artillery. *Companion of the Order of SS. Michael and George.*

Major T. Carson, Royal Irish Regiment (Garrison Battalion).

Brigadier-General V. T. Bailey, 11th Battalion King's Liverpool Regiment. *Distinguished Service Order. Mentioned in Despatches. Brevet Lieutenant-Colonel for Distinguished Services. Companion of the Order of SS. Michael and George. Wounded.*

Captain E. W. Anketell-Jones, 13th Battalion West Yorkshire Regiment.

1880.

Colonel R. E. P. Gabbet, Royal Welsh Fusiliers. *Mentioned in Despatches. Brevet Lieutenant-Colonel for Distinguished Services. Killed in action May, 1915.*

Brigadier-General H. E. Walshe, Commanding 27th Brigade. *Companion of the Order of SS. Michael and George. Mentioned in Despatches.*

Lieutenant-Colonel A. V. Alexander, 74th Punjabis, Indian Army.

Rev. C. Macan Rice, Chaplain to the Forces.

1. JOHN HENRY LOFTUS READE (1895). 2. CUTHBERT JOHN HAMILTON CLIBBORN (1895).
3. HUGH CATHCART DOBBS (1895). 4. CECIL HAMILTON CLIBBORN (1896).

1881.

Brigadier-General A. W. F. Knox, late British Military Attaché with the Russian Army, and now in Command of the British Military Mission to Siberia. *Companion of the Order of the Bath. Companion of the Order of SS. Michael and George. Companion of 3rd Class of Order of St. Vladimir, and of the 2nd Class of the Order of St. Anne, and of the 1st and 2nd Classes of the Order of St. Stanislaus. Brevet Lieutenant-Colonel and Colonel for Distinguished Services. Croix d'Officier du Légion d'Honneur.*

Colonel R. S. Hamilton, Army Ordnance Department. *Distinguished Service Order. Companion of the Order of SS. Michael and George. Three times mentioned in Despatches.*

Major A. O. Jacob, 20th Hussars.

Captain G. W. Kendall, Royal Army Medical Corps.

1882.

Brigadier-General C. W. Gwynn, C.M.G., D.S.O., Royal Engineers, General Staff Officer, 1st Grade. *Companion of the Order of the Bath. Four times mentioned in Despatches. Brevet Lieutenant-Colonel and Colonel for Distinguished Services. Croix d'Officier du Légion d'Honneur. Croix de Guerre (Belge). Wounded.*

Major G. W. R. Stacpoole, D.S.O., Assistant Provost Marshal, 5th Corps. *Officer of the Order of the British Empire (Mil. Div.). Chevalier de l'Ordre de Léopold. Croix de Guerre. Three times mentioned in Despatches. Wounded.*

Captain S. Anketell-Jones, Officer in Charge, Army Service Corps, Cork District.

Major W. A. Hardy, 5th Battalion Royal Irish Rifles.

Major C. H. Guinness, 22nd Company Royal Engineers.

Major H. S. Orpen, 16th Battalion Hampshire Regiment.

1883.

Brigadier-General H. H. S. Knox, Northamptonshire Regiment. Brigadier-General, General Staff 15th Army Corps. *Companion of the Order of the Bath. Distinguished Service Order. Croix d'Officier du Légion d'Honneur. Croix de Guerre. Brevet Lieutenant-Colonel and Colonel for Distinguished Services. Seven times mentioned in Despatches. Wounded.*

Major T. Ormsby, Army Pay Department. *Distinguished Service Order.*

1885.

Captain J. H. Brennan, 1st Battalion Royal Welsh Fusiliers. *Killed in action 19th October, 1914.*

Major C. R. W. Spedding, D.S.O., 2nd Battalion Royal Irish Rifles. *Mentioned in Despatches. Killed in action 14th September, 1914.*

Lieutenant-Colonel E. J. Jameson, 5th Battalion Leinster Regiment (S.R.) (attached Essex Regiment). *Distinguished Service Order. Killed in action 27th March, 1917.*

Lieutenant-Colonel H. S. Anderson, Royal Army Medical Corps. Commanding Hospital Ship "Britannic." *Mentioned in Despatches.*

Captain F. E. Christian, 4th Battalion Cheshire Regiment.

1. EDWARD GEORGE HARVEY (1897). 2. HUGH GORDON STAMPER (1897).
3. JOHN HENRY NUNN (1899). 4. EDMUND FITZGERALD SMYTH (1899).

1886.

Captain G. Knaggs, 4th Battalion Royal Inniskilling Fusiliers (North Coast Defence, Ireland).

1887.

Captain A. B. E. Hillas, 1/7th Battalion Gordon Highlanders. *Killed in action 23rd April, 1917.*

Gunner F. W. Hutchinson, South Africa Heavy Artillery.

Major M. L. Ferrar, Reserve of Officers, Deputy Assistant Adjutant and Quarter-Master General. Chief Censor at Bombay.

1888.

Captain C. O. Slacke, 14th Battalion Royal Irish Rifles. *Killed in action, 1st July, 1916.*

Lieutenant R. G. D. Traill, South African Remount Department. *Died of illness contracted while on active service.*

Major J. de V. Bowles, commanding 110th Brigade Royal Field Artillery. *Distinguished Service Order. Four times mentioned in Despatches.*

Major R. H. Metge, 5th Battalion Leinster Regiment.

1889.

Captain J. R. Monsell, 12th Battalion City of London Regiment (The Rangers).

Captain R. K. G. Graves, Royal Army Medical Corps.

1890.

Lieutenant-Colonel W. I. Thompson, Royal Army Medical Corps. *Distinguished Service Order. Mentioned in Despatches.*

1892.

Second Lieutenant J. R. Shaw, 9th Battalion Cheshire Regiment. *Killed in action 23rd February, 1916.*

Major W. M. Shaw, Royal Field Artillery. *Distinguished Service Order. Mentioned in Despatches. Killed in action 28th May, 1917.*

Lieutenant H. M. D. Townshend, Royal Army Medical Corps.

Lieutenant H. W. R. Blakeney, Cavalry Reserve.

Second Lieutenant S. de la P. Beresford, Anti-Aircraft Service, Royal Garrison Artillery.

Major A. G. Leech, Royal Field Artillery, serving on the Staff as Deputy-Assistant Adjutant-General. *Distinguished Service Order.*

Rev. H. B. Mayne, Chaplain Royal Navy.

Lieutenant A. E. Hamilton, Reserve of Officers, Railway Staff Officer.

Captain R. C. Metge, 5th Battalion Leinster Regiment.

Captain W. M. Crofton, Royal Army Medical Corps.

1893.

Captain A. U. O'Brien, Royal Field Artillery. *Killed in action 1st November, 1914.*

Second Lieutenant R. H. Gregg, 22nd (Service) Battalion Royal Fusiliers. *Military Cross.*

Captain S. G. S. Haughton, Indian Medical Service (attached 66th Punjabis).

Lieutenant R. F. Goodman, Northumberland Hussars.

Captain T. Henshaw, Army Service Corps.

Captain J. F. W. Leech, Royal Army Medical Corps. *Mentioned in Despatches.*

Captain R. J. G. Stoker, 1st Battalion Durham Light Infantry.

1. GEORGE WILLIAM LAWDER (1899). 2. JOHN DAVIE SCOTT (1900).
3. ARTHUR HENRY PATTERSON (1900). 4. ROBERT BURTON BENISON (1901).

Captain A. H. B. Hamilton, 4th Battalion Royal Inniskilling Fusiliers.

Captain F. R. Savage, 2nd Battalion Cheshire Regiment. *Wounded.*

Major P. G. Maynard, Royal Irish Rifles. *Distinguished Service Order. Mentioned in Despatches. Order of the Nile, 4th Class.*

Sergeant J. G. Devenish, 5th New Zealand Re-inforcements. *Twice wounded.*

Major D. M. Patrickson, 86th Carnatic Infantry, Indian Army.

Lieutenant L. P. Graves, King's Own Scottish Borderers.

Major G. T. Savage, Army Service Corps. *Distinguished Service Order. Mentioned in Despatches.*

Captain O. H. C. Molony, 94th Russell's Infantry, Indian Army.

Lieutenant J. S. Hunt, Royal Munster Fusiliers.

Platoon Sergeant A. Palmer, Malay States Volunteer Militia.

Rev. J. L. Robinson, Chaplain, Royal Navy.

Lieutenant C. H. Hayes-Hillas, Army Service Corps.

Second Lieutenant R. W. Lefroy, Motor Transport, Army Service Corps.

Captain Sir Stanley Cochrane, Bart., 7th Battalion Royal Dublin Fusiliers.

Rev. A. W. Barton, Chaplain to the Forces.

1894.

Second Lieutenant V. A. Barton, Royal Field Artillery, *Killed in action 22nd September, 1917.*

Captain C. E. Barton, 4th Battalion Royal Irish Rifles. *Killed in action 23rd August, 1918.*

Lieutenant-Colonel A. G. Rolleston, A Battery Royal Field Artillery, 171st Brigade. *Mentioned in Despatches. Brevet Lieutenant-Colonel.*

Captain D. L. Robinson, Tank Corps. *Distinguished Service Order. Croix de Guerre (with palms). Mentioned in Despatches. Wounded.*

Captain C. A. J. Vernon, Irish Guards (S. R.), attached 1st Battalion. *Military Cross.*

Lieutenant-Colonel B. B. Crozier, Royal Field Artillery. Deputy-Assistant Adjutant-General to the 13th Army Corps. *Distinguished Service Order. Three times mentioned in Despatches. Brevet Lieutenant-Colonel for Distinguished Services. Officer of the Order of the Crown of Italy. Companion of the Order of SS. Michael and George. Croix de Chevalier du Légion d'Honneur. Wounded.*

Captain C. J. F. Leech, Adjutant 15th Brigade Royal Field Artillery.

Major R. G. D. O'Callaghan, 5th Reserve Brigade Royal Field Artillery. *Member of the Order of the British Empire (Civil Div.).*

Captain D. de C. MacGillicuddy, 3rd Battalion Royal Irish Fusiliers.

Captain C. L. O'Callaghan, 8th Brigade, Ammunition Column, Royal Field Artillery.

Major E. A. W. Turbett, Canadian Overseas Railway Construction Corps. *Mentioned in Despatches.*

Staff-Sergeant H. C. Rolleston, Australian Expeditionary Force. *Wounded.*

Second Lieutenant H. F. Carroll, Royal Engineers. *Military Cross. Wounded.*

Lieutenant A. V. Macan, 29th Royal Canadians. *Wounded.*

Captain H. Freeth, Royal Army Medical Corps (attached 4th Divisional Ammunition Column).

1895.

Captain T. V. T. Thacker Neville, 3rd Dragoon Guards. *Killed in action 13th May, 1915.*

Lieutenant J. H. L. Reade, 2nd Battalion Manchester Regiment. *Mentioned in Despatches. Killed in action 29th October, 1914.*

1. ARTHUR HILL NEALE (1901). 2. WILLIAM GASTON BOYD (1901).
3. CHARLES JAMES W. K. LENDRUM (1901). 4. GEORGE AVERELL READ (1901).

Captain C. J. H. Clibborn, Brigade Major Royal Horse Artillery. *Twice mentioned in Despatches. Killed in action 14th December, 1915.*

Captain H. C. Dobbs, 124th Baluchistan Infantry, Indian Army, Commanding Somaliland Indian Contingent, King's African Rifles. *Mentioned in Despatches. Killed in action 25th May, 1918.*

Lieutenant-Colonel R. E. U. Newman, Royal Army Medical Corps. *Mentioned in Despatches. Military Cross.*

Captain F. R. Seymour, Royal Army Medical Corps.

Lieutenant T. R. Beaumont, Loyal North Lancashire Regiment.

Lieutenant W. H. Hutchinson, North Irish Horse (attached Royal Irish Fusiliers). *Wounded.*

Major R. L. Payne, 1st Battalion Connaught Rangers. *Distinguished Service Order. Mentioned in Despatches.*

Lieutenant-Colonel E. C. Phelan, Royal Army Medical Corps. *Distinguished Service Order. Military Cross. Twice mentioned in Despatches.*

Major S. W. S. Hamilton, 70th Field Company Royal Engineers. *Distinguished Service Order. Mentioned in Despatches. Bar to Distinguished Service Order.*

Major B. C. A. Leeper, New Zealand Medical Staff Corps (attached 4th Waikato Mounted Rifles).

Lieutenant M. B. Lendrum, Brigade Machine Gun Company, Ulster Division. *Wounded.*

Corporal J. S. Miller, 20th Battalion Royal Fusiliers (Transport Section).

Major H. F. V. Greer, Royal Garrison Artillery.

Captain N. E. Drury, 6th Battalion Royal Dublin Fusiliers.

Lieutenant-Colonel C. R. M. Morris, Royal Army Medical Corps. *Distinguished Service Order. Twice mentioned in Despatches.*

1896.

Captain C. H. Clibborn, 92nd Punjabis. *Killed in action 10th April, 1916.*

Major P. G. Pratt, Royal Field Artillery.

Captain C. S. Hamilton, Leinster Regiment. *Wounded.*

Major F. L. Robinson, Commanding 63rd Squadron Royal Flying Corps. *Brevet-Major for Distinguished Services. Distinguished Service Order. Military Cross. Mentioned in Despatches.*

Captain A. Creery, 110th Heavy Battery Royal Garrison Artillery. *Twice mentioned in Depatches. Military Cross.*

Captain A. H. Peyton, 13th Rajputs, Indian Army.

Captain L. T. H. Leland, 10th Battalion Worcestershire Regiment. *Wounded.*

Lieutenant J. A. Powell, Royal Army Medical Corps.

Second Lieutenant H. B. Bennett, 2nd Queen's Own Sappers and Miners, Royal Engineers.

Second Lieutenant H. J. D. Stokes, Army Service Corps.

Second Lieutenant G. A. H. Hone, 6th Battalion Royal Irish Regiment.

N. C. Whitton, Local Volunteer Force, S. Wynaad, India.

Rev. J. H. Stanton, Hospital Orderly, Anglo-Belgian Hospital, France.

Captain T. W. Bridge, Chota Nagpur Light Horse.

1897.

Captain E. G. Harvey, 1st Battalion Wiltshire Regiment and Royal Flying Corps. *Killed in action 16th June, 1915.*

Lance-Corporal H. G. Stamper, 10th Battalion Royal Dublin Fusiliers. *Killed in action 13th November, 1916.*

1. GEORGE GUY FINLAY (1903). 2. ROBERT ALEXANDER FINLAY (1904).
3. RALPH WILLIAM G. HINDS (1905). 4. PERCY THOMAS JORDAN (1905).

Lieutenant-Colonel J. du P. Langrishe, Royal Army Medical Corps, Commanding No. 12 Ambulance. *Distinguished Service Order. Mentioned in Despatches.*

Captain P. R. Jordi, 109th Company, Royal Engineers.

Lieutenant R. J. Mills, Army Service Corps.

Second Lieutenant W. H. Kennedy, 4th Battalion Leinster Regiment.

Lieutenant J. B. de W. Molony, Indian Medical Service.

Lieutenant R. H. B. de la P. Beresford, 1st Battalion Royal Dublin Fusiliers.

Rev. W. L. R. Bourchier, Chaplain to the Forces. Resigned.

Major J. W. Seigne, Royal Marine Light Infantry. (General Staff Officer, 2nd Grade). *Promoted Major "for Brilliant Service."*

Captain T. R. B. Seigne, Royal Field Artillery. *Mentioned in Despatches. Military Cross. Croix de Guerre.*

Lieutenant M. Dockrell, 116th Mahrattas, Indian Army.

Captain F. Bantry White, Auxiliary Horse Transport Company, Army Service Corps. *Military Cross.*

Captain A. E. J. Croly, 11th Battalion Australian Imperial Force. *Mentioned in Despatches. Wounded.*

Captain E. P. G. Bridge, 6th Battalion Royal Irish Regiment. *Wounded.*

1898.

Captain C. H. M. Furnell, Royal Garrison Artillery. *Killed in action 30th April, 1916.*

Lieutenant G. R. Stanton, Army Service Corps.

Captain R. B. Langrishe, Supply and Transport Corps, Indian Army.

Lieutenant A. H. Pemberton, Royal Army Medical Corps.

Lieutenant G. M. Mayberry, Royal Army Medical Corps.

Captain G. B. Newcomen, 2nd Battalion East Lancashire Regiment. *Wounded.*

Captain J. C. Tate, 127th (Q. M. O.) Baluchistan Light Infantry.

Captain E. F. Lawson, Royal Army Medical Corps (attached 7th Labour Group, Headquarters).

1899.

Major J. H. Nunn, Commanding A Battery, 149th Brigade Royal Field Artillery. *Mentioned in Despatches. Killed in action 1st April, 1917.*

Major E. F. Smyth, 11th Battalion Royal Irish Rifles. *Military Cross. Killed in action 3rd December, 1917.*

Lieutenant G. W. D. Lawder, Trench Mortar Battery, 1st Brigade, Canadian Expeditionary Force. *Killed in action 27th September, 1918.*

Major C. G. Place, 8th Battalion East Surrey Regiment. *Distinguished Service Order. Military Cross. Wounded.*

Lieutenant A. E. A. M. Munn, 11th Battalion Royal Inniskilling Fusiliers.

Lieutenant L. O. M. Munn, 11th Battalion Royal Inniskilling Fusiliers.

Private S. G. Powell, 1st Battalion Honourable Artillery Company.

Captain B. C. Powell, Royal Army Medical Corps.

Captain W. A. Lane, Army Service Corps (attached 53rd Brigade Royal Garrison Artillery). *Twice mentioned in Despatches. Military Cross.*

Captain E. P. Yeates, 1/12th Pioneers, Indian Army.

Sergeant E. A. Atkinson, C. Battalion Canadian Mounted Rifles, 3rd Canadian Contingent.

1. HUGH A. H. WARNOCK (1905). 2. HASTINGS G. KILLINGLEY (1905).
3. WILLIAM GEORGE M. EAGAR (1906). 4. JAMES N. H. MURPHY (1906).

Captain G. C. King, Royal Army Medical Corps (attached Heavy Artillery).

Second Lieutenant A. W. Lepper, King's Shropshire Light Infantry.

Captain G. B. Read, 36th Siege Battery Royal Garrison Artillery.

Second Lieutenant G. M. Gordon, Royal Engineers.

Captain J. S. Smith, Royal Army Medical Corps (Dental Department).

1900.

Lieutenant-Colonel J. D. Scott, Commanding 3rd Battalion Royal Irish Regiment. *Distinguished Service Order. Killed in action 21st March, 1918.*

Second Lieutenant A. H. Patterson, 9th Battalion Royal Inniskilling Fusiliers. *Killed in action 14th October, 1918.*

Captain D. L. J. Babington, 6th Divisional Ammunition Column, Motor Transport Department, Army Service Corps. *Twice mentioned in Despatches.*

Captain A. W. Galwey, Royal Irish Rifles. *Wounded.*

Lieutenant S. S. Payne, 4th Battalion Royal Munster Fusiliers (attached Royal Fusiliers). *Wounded.*

Second Lieutenant T. F. M. Greene, Motor Transport, Army Service Corps.

Lieutenant H. F. Blood, Royal Army Medical Corps.

Captain G. B. Long, 4th Battalion Royal Dublin Fusiliers (attached 9th Battalion).

Lieutenant F. P. H. Bull, 1st Battalion Royal Inniskilling Fusiliers. *Wounded.*

Lieutenant A. S. Duggan, Mechanical Transport Department, Army Service Corps. *Mentioned in Despatches.*

Lieutenant H. Fleming, Royal Army Medical Corps.

1901.

Second Lieutenant R. B. Benison, 2nd Battalion Connaught Rangers. *Killed in action 20th September, 1914.*

Lieutenant A. H. Neale, 1st Brahmans, Indian Army. *Killed in action 21st January, 1916.*

Second Lieutenant W. G. Boyd, Royal Inniskilling Fusiliers. *Killed in action 13th October, 1916.*

Major C. J. W. K. Lendrum, 3rd Battalion Royal Inniskilling Fusiliers (attached 1st Battalion). *Mentioned in Despatches. Killed in action 13th November, 1916.*

Captain G. A. Read, 3rd Battalion Leinster Regiment. *Killed in action 8th March, 1917.*

Lieutenant-Commander C. H. Rolleston, Royal Navy.

Captain J. E. Richey, 76th Field Company, Royal Engineers. *Military Cross. Wounded.*

Major G. J. L. Stoney, Worcestershire Regiment. *Distinguished Service Order. Military Cross.*

Second Lieutenant H. M. Read, 2nd Life Guards.

Second Lieutenant A. J. D. Henry, Royal Field Artillery. *Wounded.*

Second Lieutenant E. L. Grimwade, 2nd Battalion Suffolk Regiment.

Private C. O. Mellor, 3rd Canadian Tunnelling Company.

1902.

Second Lieutenant G. F. Nixon, Royal Field Artillery. *Mentioned in Despatches. Killed in action 24th October, 1914.*

Captain J. W. Battersby, Royal Field Artillery. *Military Cross. Twice mentioned in Despatches. Killed in action.*

1. RICHARD P. HEMPHILL (1906). 2. ALFRED FRANCIS BATE (1907).
3. GEORGE NEVILLE PATRICK YOUNG (1907). 4. ARTHUR CHICHESTER CROOKSHANK (1907).

Second Lieutenant M. E. F. B. Jameson, 5th Battalion (attached 2nd Battalion) Royal Dublin Fusiliers. *Wounded.*

Lieutenant R. C. Nixon, 1st Battalion Norfolk Regiment (attached 5th Signal Company Royal Engineers). *Mentioned in Despatches. Wounded.*

Private G. E. Scharff, Royal Engineers.

Lieutenant F. J. H. McCormick, 3rd Battalion Royal Dublin Fusiliers (attached 1st Battalion). *Wounded.*

Captain G. H. Barry, 5th Battalion Leinster Regiment (attached Royal Air Force).

Second Lieutenant W. B. Close, Royal Engineers.

1903.

Lieutenant G. G. Finlay, Royal Irish Regiment. *Killed in action July, 1916.*

Lieutenant R. C. Young, Royal Naval Volunteer Reserve.

Second Lieutenant G. Watt, 1018 Company A.S.C. (Mechanical Transport Service).

First Sergeant H. V. Stanton, 26th Hospital Train, United States Army.

1904.

Lieutenant R. A. Finlay, 5th Battalion Royal Dublin Fusiliers (attached 1st Battalion Royal Irish Rifles). *Killed in action 9th May, 1915.*

Captain T. A. Lawder, 6th Field Ambulance, Royal Army Medical Corps. *Mentioned in Despatches.*

Captain F. S. Gillespie, 49th Field Ambulance, Royal Army Medical Corps.

Captain M. G. Young, 2/6th Battalion South Staffordshire Regiment.

1905.

Lieutenant R. W. G. Hinds, 2nd Battalion Royal Inniskilling Fusiliers. *Mentioned in Despatches. Killed in action 16th May, 1915.*

Second Lieutenant P. T. Jordan, 1st Battalion Royal Inniskilling Fusiliers. *Killed in action 21st August, 1915.*

Lieutenant H. A. H. Warnock, 4th Battalion Royal Irish Fusiliers (attached 1st Battalion). *Killed in action 16th August, 1915.*

Second Lieutenant H. G. Killingley, Royal Dublin Fusiliers. *Killed in action 23rd October, 1916.*

Captain R. A. J. Goff, Army Service Corps.

Major G. A. Bridge, Royal Army Medical Corps, 11th Field Ambulance. *Military Cross.*

Captain W. A. G. Hinds, 103rd Mahratta Light Infantry. *Military Cross. Mentioned in Despatches. Wounded.*

Lieutenant H. F. Otway, Leinster Regiment (attached Army Cyclist Corps). *Military Cross. Mentioned in Despatches. Wounded.*

Lieutenant S. V. Furlong, Royal Army Medical Corps.

R. S. S. Treanor, General Inspecting Officer, Circle 4, Board of Ordnance, India.

Captain C. C. Barry, 2nd Battalion Leinster Regiment (attached Royal Air Force). *Military Cross. Wounded.*

Corporal O. A. Barry, 63rd Battalion Canadian Expeditionary Force. *Wounded.*

Lieutenant A. E. G. Bailey, Army Service Corps (attached Royal Flying Corps).

Private R. F. Peet, 6th Battalion The Buffs.

Second Lieutenant P. A. Bell, Royal Garrison Artillery.

Pilot R. I. M. Hitchcock, Canadian Royal Flying Corps.

1. ERNEST DICKINSON PRICE (1907). 2. ERIC EDGE BEATTY (1908).
3. LAWRENCE HILL WILLSON M'KISACK (1908). 4. JOHN HULEATT REVINGTON (1908).

1906.

Captain W. G. M. Eagar, 3rd Battalion Royal Munster Fusiliers (attached 1st Battalion). *Killed in action 21st August, 1915.*

Second Lieutenant J. N. H. Murphy, Royal Dublin Fusiliers. *Killed in action 10th May, 1915.*

Second Lieutenant R. P. Hemphill, Leinster Regiment and Royal Flying Corps. *Killed in action 24th March, 1917.*

Surgeon-Lieutenant A. H. Price, Royal Navy.

Captain A. H. Wilson, 4th Battalion Royal Irish Fusiliers.

Second Lieutenant I. K. Price, Army Service Corps. *Wounded.*

Bombardier P. A. Thunder, 1st Battery Canadian Artillery. *Twice wounded.*

Second Lieutenant H. Crookshank, Royal Engineers. *Mentioned in Despatches. Wounded.*

Second Lieutenant T. F. Webb, Royal Fusiliers. *Missing.*

Lieutenant C. G. Price, 2nd Battalion Royal Irish Regiment. *Wounded.*

Captain M. F. Bridge, Army Service Corps (attached Royal Flying Corps). *Wounded.*

Major J. W. Hughes, Royal Field Artillery. *Military Cross. Wounded.*

Second Lieutenant I. R. Gillespie, 15th Battalion Royal Irish Rifles. *Wounded.*

Private G. C. Johnston, Army Service Corps.

Surgeon-Sub-Lieutenant F. McG. Ferguson, Royal Navy.

Private B. F. Bridge, Malay States Volunteers.

Second Lieutenant J. W. Q. Day, 4th Battalion Royal Munster Fusiliers (attached Royal Irish Regiment).

1907.

Second Lieutenant A. F. Bate, Royal Dublin Fusiliers (attached 2nd Battalion Leinster Regiment). *Killed in action 14th March, 1915.*

Lieutenant G. N. P. Young, 2nd Battalion Leinster Regiment. *Military Cross. Mentioned in Despatches. Killed in action 25th July, 1915.*

Sergeant A. C. Crookshank, 7th Battalion Royal Dublin Fusiliers. *Distinguished Conduct Medal. Killed in action 16th August, 1915.*

Lieutenant E. D. Price, 3rd Battalion Royal Irish Regiment (attached 2nd Battalion). *Killed in action 19th March, 1916.*

Flight-Commander G. W. Price, Royal Naval Air Service. *Bar to Distinguished Service Cross. Missing.*

Captain E. R. Greer, 106th Hazara Pioneers, Indian Army. *Twice mentioned in Despatches.*

Lieutenant W. E. CaldBeck, Royal Dublin Fusiliers. *Wounded.*

Surgeon-Sub-Lieutenant J. W. Scharff, Royal Naval Volunteer Reserve. *Invalided, with retention of rank.*

Second Lieutenant R. A. Yeates, 3rd Battalion Royal Dublin Fusiliers.

Second Lieutenant K. K. O'Connor, 14th (K. G. O.) Ferozepore Sikhs. *Wounded.*

Private N. A. Austin, Canadian Expeditionary Force.

1908.

Lieutenant E. E. Beatty, 6th Battalion Connaught Rangers. *Killed in action 29th April, 1916.*

Second Lieutenant L. H. W. M'Kisack, 5th Lancers and Royal Flying Corps. *Killed in action 13th November, 1916.*

1. GEORGE R. L. BAILLIE (1908). 2. FREDERICK GIBSON HEUSTON (1909).
3. FRANCIS ROBERT HEUSTON (1909). 4. ALFRED M. B. B. ROSE-CLELAND (1909).

Second Lieutenant J. H. Revington, 9th Battalion Devonshire Regiment. *Killed in action 4th September, 1916.*

Lieutenant G. R. L. Baillie, 4th Battalion Royal Inniskilling Fusiliers. *Mentioned in Despatches. Killed in action 3rd October, 1918.*

Captain D. Beatty, 8th Battalion Royal Dublin Fusiliers.

Lieutenant G. A. Todd, 3rd Battalion Leinster Regiment (attached 2nd Battalion). *Wounded.*

Private J. D. Watson, South Irish Horse.

Lieutenant G. O. Young, 11th Battalion Royal Irish Rifles. *Gas Poisoning.*

Captain A. V. Bridge, 6th Battalion Royal Irish Regiment. *Three times wounded.*

Second Lieutenant H. Crosbie, 3rd Battalion Royal Dublin Fusiliers. *Wounded.*

Lieutenant G. V. G. Beamish, Royal Naval Reserve.

Captain G. Y. Tyrrell, Royal Air Force. *Military Cross. Wounded.*

Second Lieutenant F. A. Newell, 5th Battalion Royal Irish Fusiliers. *Twice wounded.*

Captain W. L. Lloyd, 7th Battalion Shropshire Light Infantry. *Military Cross.*

Corporal G. M. Beere, 5th Battalion Gloucester Regiment. Resigned through ill health.

Lieutenant N. G. Ball, 8th Battalion Royal Dublin Fusiliers. *Wounded.*

Second Lieutenant J. E. Beatty, Royal Field Artillery. *Wounded.*

Corporal H. S. Barton, Inland Water Transport, Royal Engineers. *Wounded.*

1909.

Second Lieutenant F. G. Heuston, 6th Battalion Royal Irish Fusiliers. *Military Cross. Mentioned in Despatches. Killed in action 16th August, 1915.*

Captain F. R. Heuston, 1st Battalion Royal Montreal Regiment, 1st Canadian Contingent. *Killed in action 8th April, 1916.*

Second Lieutenant A. M. B. B. Rose-Cleland, 1st Battalion Royal Dublin Fusiliers. *Killed in action 1st July, 1916.*

Second Lieutenant F. B. Falkiner, Royal Irish Rifles and Royal Flying Corps. *Military Cross. The King of Italy's Bronze Medal for Military Valour. Killed in action 21st August, 1917.*

Second Lieutenant H. S. M. M'Entire, 5th Battalion South Hampshire Regiment.

Lieutenant C. H. Stewart, 106th Hazara Pioneers, Indian Army.

Captain P. Stephens, 4th Battalion Royal Dublin Fusiliers. *Mentioned in Despatches.*

Second Lieutenant A. H. Stephens, 4th Battalion Royal Dublin Fusiliers. Resigned through ill health.

Second Lieutenant R. G. Price, Royal Field Artillery.

Captain T. F. Given, 9th Battalion Royal Irish Fusiliers. *Military Cross. Mentioned in Despatches. Three times wounded.*

Second Lieutenant L. MacG. Dillon, Royal Garrison Artillery.

Second Lieutenant W. M. Gibbon, Army Service Corps.

Second Lieutenant J. K. B. Coghill, 3rd Battalion South Wales Borderers.

Lieutenant W. M. M. Elvery, 5th Battalion Royal Inniskilling Fusiliers (attached 1st Battalion). *Twice wounded.*

1. FREDERICK B. FALKINER (1909). 2. OSBORNE SAMUEL BURKE (1910).
3. WILLIAM PEDLOW (1911). 4. ADAM CYRIL D. HILL (1911).

Second Lieutenant F. G. Stewart, attached to 55th (Cokes) Rifles, Indian Army.

Second Lieutenant C. J. G. Conerney. *Wounded.*

1910.

Second Lieutenant O. S. Burke, Royal Field Artillery. *Killed in action November, 1916.*

Lieutenant R. N. Nunn, Indian Cavalry. *Military Cross.*

Captain C. B. Forde, 46th Brigade Royal Field Artillery. *Mentioned in Despatches. Wounded.*

Lieutenant C. A. Galt-Gamble, 1st Battalion Royal Dublin Fusiliers (attached 1st Battalion Connaught Rangers). *Twice wounded.*

Captain R. G. Lewis, 6th Battalion Leinster Regiment. *Mentioned in Despatches.*

Lieutenant R. D. Greer, 7th Battalion Royal Irish Fusiliers. *Wounded.*

Captain J. E. H. Gelston, 1st Lancers, Indian Army.

Lieutenant W. E. C. Moore, 2/1st Lowland Brigade Royal Field Artillery.

Second Lieutenant H. C. Charles, 4th Battalion Royal Irish Rifles.

Second Lieutenant M. St. G. C. Johnston, Indian Army Reserve of Officers (No. 1 Mechanical Transport Company).

Second Lieutenant H. S. Robinson, 1st Reserve Cavalry. *Distinguished Conduct Medal. Wounded.*

T. F. L. Cary, Royal Naval Auxiliary Sick Berth Reserve.

Second Lieutenant A. H. Montgomery, 3rd (S.R.) Battalion Royal Irish Regiment (attached 12th Battalion Royal Irish Rifles). *Wounded.*

Lieutenant H. T. Gilchrist, Army Service Corps. *Mentioned in Despatches.*

Second Lieutenant A. D. K. Perkins, Royal Irish Fusiliers and Royal Flying Corps.

Midshipman F. W. Haughton, Royal Navy.

Lieutenant R. L. Murray, Royal Garrison Artillery. *Military Cross and Bar.*

Second Lieutenant R. C. Pigott, Royal Flying Corps.

Second Lieutenant A. G. L. Sidwell, 1st Battalion Royal Dublin Fusiliers (attached Royal Flying Corps).

Second Lieutenant W. S. Moore, Indian Army.

W. R. Aykroyd, Cadet, Royal Air Force.

H. E. Bell, Cadet, the Artists' Rifles Officers' Training Corps.

1911.

Captain W. Pedlow, Royal Dublin Fusiliers. *Parchment Certificate. Military Cross. Twice mentioned in Despatches. Killed in action 12th October, 1918.*

Second Lieutenant A. C. D. Hill, 4th Battalion Royal Irish Rifles (attached 7th Battalion). *Parchment Certificate for gallant conduct and devotion to duty. Killed in action 16th August, 1917.*

Lieutenant C. Campbell, Headquarters' Staff.

Second Lieutenant N. V. Taylor, 2/4th King's African Rifles. *Twice wounded.*

Private E. Hamilton, British Columbia Horse. *Wounded.*

Lieutenant F. M. Moore, 52nd Sikhs. *Wounded.*

Bombardier J. Sibley, Royal Field Artillery.

J. P. Phipps, Gentleman Cadet, Indian Army.

Second Lieutenant R. H. Maunsell-Eyre, 2nd Battalion Royal Munster Fusiliers.

Private G. W. S. Warnock, Royal Irish Regiment.

Lieutenant W. S. Seymour, Army Service Corps. *Wounded.*

Private P. B. Pierce, 4th Battalion Royal Fusiliers.

1. EDWARD BENJAMIN B. WILLIAMSON (1912). 2. GERALD SOMERVILLE YEATS CULLEN (1912).
3. LUDLOW NORMAN JONES (1912). 4. LAURENCE ELVIDGE (1913).

Second Lieutenant A. B. L. Lawson, Machine Gun Corps, 61st Company.

Sapper (Interpreter) R. V. Litton, Royal Engineers. *Gassed. Wounded.*

Lieutenant W. R. G. Dowd, Royal Garrison Artillery.

Second Lieutenant N. Manly, 3rd (S.R.) Battalion Royal Irish Regiment. *Wounded.*

Second Lieutenant W. V. C. Maffett, Royal Garrison Artillery.

Sergeant F. W. Hyde, 3rd Battalion Honourable Artillery Company.

Second Lieutenant N. R. Scully, Royal Flying Corps.

Second Lieutenant H. J. Delmege, 1st Reserve Regiment of Lancers.

1912.

Second Lieutenant E. B. B. Williamson, 3rd Battalion Connaught Rangers. *Killed in action 19th February, 1917.*

Second Lieutenant G. S. Y. Cullen, 1st Battalion (attached 3rd Battalion) Royal Irish Fusiliers. *Killed in action 11th April, 1917.*

Lieutenant L. N. Jones, 9th Battalion South Wales Borderers (attached Royal Air Force). *Killed in action 3rd October, 1918.*

Captain L. H. Beresford-Poer, 59th Battery Royal Field Artillery.

Second Lieutenant C. W. Scott, 3rd Battalion Royal Irish Regiment. *Wounded.*

Lieutenant D. F. W. Warren, 5th Battalion Royal Munster Fusiliers (attached 1/12th Pioneers, Indian Army).

Lieutenant C. S. Marriott, 16th Battalion Lancashire Fusiliers. *Wounded.*

Lieutenant T. M. N. Guilford, Royal Garrison Artillery.

Lieutenant D. B. Maffett, 31st Punjabis, Indian Army.

Second Lieutenant V. W. Gamble, 1st Garrison Battalion Royal Munster Fusiliers.

Second Lieutenant R. M. Davies, 104th Wellesley's Rifles, Indian Army.

Surgeon-Sub-Lieutenant C. E. McQuade, Royal Naval Volunteer Reserve.

E. P. S. Shirley, Gentleman Cadet, Sandhurst.

Second Lieutenant E. W. Thornley, 1st Battalion Royal Munster Fusiliers (from Sandhurst).

1913.

Second Lieutenant L. Elvidge, 5th Battalion Connaught Rangers. *Killed in action 9th August, 1916.*

H. C. Kennedy, Cadet, Royal Field Artillery. *Died of illness contracted while on active service.*

Lieutenant N. F. Hone, 3rd Battalion Royal Irish Rifles (attached 9th Battalion). *Killed in action.*

Lieutenant B. A. Ryan, 1st Battalion 4th Ghurkha Rifles.

Lieutenant J. D. Woodall, Royal Garrison Artillery. *Military Cross.*

Second Lieutenant J. J. Fitzgerald, 120th Rajputs, Indian Army.

Second Lieutenant E. L'E. Davies, Royal Garrison Artillery.

C. A. Richardson, Cadet, Dublin University Officers' Training Corps.

Midshipman G. R. Deverell, Royal Navy.

Second Lieutenant N. McKenny, 1st Battalion Royal Irish Fusiliers.

E. F. C. Hardman, Gentleman Cadet, Indian Army.

Second Lieutenant G. T. Pearson, 58th Regiment (Vaughan's Rifles) Indian Army.

1. HERBERT COLLES KENNEDY (1913).
2. NATHANIEL FREDERICK HONE (1913).

Second Lieutenant C. L. Barcroft, Royal Marine Light Infantry.

R. S. Shuel, Cadet, Dublin University Officers' Training Corps.

K. D. B. Dobbs, Cadet, Dublin University Officers' Training Corps.

1914.

G. G. M. Symes, Cadet, Royal Air Force.

Sapper J. G. King, Despatch Rider, Royal Engineers.

G. R. O'N. Moriarty, Gentleman Cadet, Indian Army.

G. Gresson, Cadet, Dublin University Officers' Training Corps.

H. R. Hopking, Gentleman Cadet, Sandhurst.

Cadet R. N. Stanton, Royal Air Force.

1915.

P. M. Goodbody, Gentleman Cadet, Sandhurst.

Lieutenant R. L. D'E. Byrn, Irish Guards.

E. A. Healy, Flight Cadet, Royal Air Force.

T. J. Shaw, Cadet, Royal Air Force.

1916.

Midshipman C. W. Huggard, Royal Navy.

H. St. G. Smith, Despatch Rider, Royal Air Force.

W. A. B. Reid, Gentleman Cadet, Sandhurst.

INDEX.

INDEX—CONTINUED.

INDEX—CONTINUED.

INDEX—CONTINUED.

INDEX—CONTINUED.

Printed by
W. WARREN & SON,
15 Lower Ormond Quay,
DUBLIN.